Presented to:

_____

A righteous man who walks in his integrity—
How blessed are his sons after him.

PROVERBS 20:7 NASB

Presented by:

_____

Date:

_____

Celebrate
Dad

Heartwarming Stories,
Inspirational Sayings, and
Loving Expressions
for a Special Father

WHITE STONE BOOKS
LAKELAND, FLORIDA

Celebrate Dad:
Heartwarming Stories, Inspirational Sayings, and Loving Expressions
for a Special Father

ISBN 1-59379-057-0

Copyright © 2006 Bordon Books, Tulsa, OK
Published by White Stone Books
P.O. Box 2835
Lakeland, Florida 33806

Manuscript written and prepared by SnapdragonGroup℠ Editorial Services

Contents

The imprint of the father
remains forever on the life of the child.

Introduction

Fatherhood is an awesome role and carries with it profound responsibility. Therefore, it is fitting that we salute and pay tribute to fathers for all they have given us. For the anchors of strength and courage we carry with us in life ... for the wisdom shared through their words and good example ... for the love and sacrifices made for their families—these are the things that define a father's success, that make him an extraordinary person and an extraordinary dad, and these are the things that deserve to be celebrated.

Whether you have been a father for many years or you are looking forward to the birth of your first child, *Celebrate Dad* was designed to inspire, encourage, and applaud the role God has placed you in—a role your Heavenly Father invented for himself and has called you to.

An Extraordinary Dad Loves from the Heart

There is something ultimate in a father's love,
something that cannot fail, something to be believed
against the whole world.

FREDERICK WILLIAM FABER
Anglican Minister and Hymn Writer
1814-1863

God is love. His nature is love. And it was that love that caused Him to create us, redeem us, and care for us. When love—the deep abiding kind rather than the superficial, permissive kind—defines you as a father, you are acting in harmony with the Heavenly Father. Though the waters may sometimes be rough, the day will come when your children will bless you.

The LORD is gracious and compassionate,
slow to anger and rich in love.

PSALM 145:8

Love feels no burden, thinks nothing of trouble,
attempts what is above its strength, pleads no excuse of
impossibility; for it thinks all things lawful for itself,
and all things possible. It is therefore able to undertake all things,
and warrants them to take effect, where he who does not love,
would faint and lie down.

THOMAS À KEMPIS
Priest, Monk, and Writer
1380-1471

Vulnerability, attachment, uprooting,
tenderness, interest, anxiety, expectation,
anguish—all these are nothing else but love.

LOUIS EVELY
Religious Writer

—⁓—

Love is watchful, humble, and upright.
Love is not fickle and sentimental, nor is it
intent on vanities. It is sober, pure, steadfast,
quiet, and guarded in all the senses.

THOMAS À KEMPIS
Priest, Monk, and Writer
1380-1471

God's Love Comes from the Heart

His love for you ...

- *is the essence of His being.* You can express God's heart to your children because you yourself have experienced that "God is love" (1 John 4:16).

- *was revealed in Christ and is not dependent on your love for Him.* Your love for your children is unconditional—not based on anything they do for you, but based on your father-child relationship. In the same way, "God's love was revealed among us in this way: God sent his only Son into the world so that we might live through him. In this is love, not that we loved God but that he loved us and sent his Son to be the atoning sacrifice for our sins" (1 John 4:9–10 NRSV).

- *cannot be taken away.* Can you imagine ever not loving your children? Neither can God imagine not loving you: "I am convinced that nothing can ever separate us from his love. Death can't, and life can't. The angels won't, and all the powers of hell itself cannot keep God's love away. Our fears for today, our worries about tomorrow, or where we are—high above the sky, or in the deepest ocean—nothing will ever be able to separate us from the love of God demonstrated by our Lord Jesus Christ when he died for us" (Romans 8:38–39 TLB).

- *makes everything right.* Just as dads know how to make things right for their kids, "God's love ... is ever and always, eternally present to all who fear him, making everything right for them and their children" (Psalm 103:17 THE MESSAGE).

We need good fathers in our homes
Whose hearts are full of grace.
Who by their love and earnest prayers,
Make home a pleasant place.

WALTER E. ISENHOUR
American Poet

F.A.T.H.E.R.S

F is for "faithful"

A is for "always there"

T is for "truthful and trustworthy"

H is for "honorable"

E is for "ever-loving"

R is for "righteous"

S is for "supportive"

*H*eavenly Father,

Help me to be a father who loves his children with all of his heart. I want my love to surround my children and cause them to feel safe and protected. When they have a challenge in life, I pray that they will run to me and that I can comfort them in the way that will benefit them most.

Lord, bless my children. Show me how to teach them in life, how to talk to You, how to strive to be the best person they can possibly be. I want to love my children the way You love me, Lord. Thank You for helping me to show my family how to live out their lives with great strength of character and absolute trust in You through personal example.

AMEN.

"It's Me! It's Me!"

When I was a child, I couldn't believe God could love me unconditionally. Maybe it was because my father, though I knew he loved me, seemed to put so many conditions on his approval. But since my own daughter was born, I have learned how a godly father should interact with his children.

"Do you love me, Daddy?" my five-year-old daughter Michelle would often ask of my husband, Richard—not because she didn't like his answer, but because she never tired of hearing his response.

"You bet! I love you very, very much!" my husband would reply, often adding a bear hug or a tickle.

In every possible way—in time spent hugging, joking, and listening to her—Richard shows Michelle how much he truly loves her.

She sees his love for her when he praises the drawing she has made for him. She sees his love when he chews a children's grape-flavored Tylenol at the same time she does, encouraging her when her fever is high and she feels sick and afraid.

She knows her daddy loves her when he repairs a toy, wipes a tear, and laughs at her knock-knock jokes. She's always secure in her daddy's love, knowing that it is never-ending, without limits, and unconditional.

Even when she's disobedient and is given a time-out or loses a privilege, Richard always says, "I still love you, Michelle. Just because I'm unhappy with something you've done, it doesn't mean I'll ever stop loving you."

As I watch my husband with our daughter, I thank God that I've been given this example of a loving father. It even changed the way I viewed God as my Heavenly Father. Whenever I see my husband interacting with my daughter, I offer up a prayer of thanks that when God is spoken of as "Father," it will bring images of love and compassion to her and a strong belief that God will love her no matter what.

One of my daughter's favorite games to play with her dad is "Guess Who I Love?" Holding her in his arms, he smiles and says, "Guess who I love?"

Michelle, with a gleam in her eye, asks, "Who?"

"Well," her father says, "this special person I really, really love has blonde hair and blue eyes."

Michelle will pat her hair and point to her eyes. "I have blonde hair and blue eyes."

Richard will nod and say, "And this special person I really, really love has a favorite color of green."

Michelle claps her hands and shouts, "My favorite color is green!"

"And, this person I really, really love is great at athletics and loves to swim."

"I do! I do!" Michelle says. By now she's hugging

herself and ready to burst with excitement.

Richard takes a deep breath. "This person I really, really love, well, her name is Michelle."

"It's me! It's me!" Michelle screams, giving her daddy a big hug.

This repeated ritual is such a simple moment, a small space of time, yet it always overwhelms Michelle with the knowledge of her father's love. A true father loves from the heart.[1]

Dad opened the jar of pickles when no one else could. He was the only one in the house who wasn't afraid to go into the basement by himself. He cut himself shaving, but no one kissed it or got excited about it. It was understood when it rained, he got the car and brought it around to the door. When anyone was sick, he went out to get the prescription filled. He took lots of pictures ... but he was never in them.

ERMA BOMBECK
American Humorist
1927-1996

My daddy doesn't work; he just goes to the office.
But sometimes he does errands on the way home.

A LITTLE GIRL

—ɷ—

My father was a quiet man.
His loving care said all that needed to be said.

A GRATEFUL SON

—ɷ—

Love does not dominate; it
cultivates.

JOHANN WOLFGANG VON GOETHE
German Poet, Novelist, and
Playwright
1749-1832

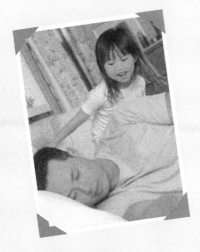

An Extraordinary Dad Is Strong and Courageous

A father is a person who is forced to
endure childbirth without an anesthetic.

PAUL HARVEY
American Radio Broadcaster
1918-

It was once important for fathers to be physically strong. They had to build homes and hunt for food with their bare hands. They were also called upon to put their physical bodies between their loved ones and predators, both animal and human. But things have changed. Now it is more important for a man to be mentally and spiritually strong, able to protect his children from assaults on their minds and their faith—dangers that most often are unseen. An extraordinary father draws his strength and courage from his moral character and relationship with God. He understands that protecting his family can no longer be done with steel abs alone.

Be on your guard; stand firm in the faith;
be men of courage; be strong.

1 CORINTHIANS 16:13

A father is the head of a unit of people

launched on an exploration of life and

all the things God has placed in the world

for us to enjoy.

GORDON MACDONALD

Scottish Novelist, Poet, Clergyman, and Author of Children's Books

1824-1905

What Makes a Dad

God took the strength of a mountain,

The majesty of a tree,

The warmth of a summer sun,

The calm of a quiet sea,

The generous soul of nature,

The comforting arm of night,

The wisdom of the ages,

The power of the eagle's flight,

The joy of a morning in spring,

The faith of a mustard seed,

The patience of eternity,

The depth of a family need.

Then God combined these qualities,

When there was nothing more to add.

He knew His masterpiece was complete,

And so,

He called it ... Dad

AUTHOR UNKNOWN

A Tribute to My Dad

My father was strong physically. I remember watching in awe as he slammed his axe into the trunk of a tree, downing it in just a few blows. But I can see now that my father was strong in other ways as well. In matters of honesty and integrity, he could not be compromised. His word was his bond. He kept his promises. And that's not all. I remember waking in the night to the sound of his voice—filled with fervor—praying for us.

I am thankful for my father's presence in my life, and it is my desire to teach my children in the same example—teaching them to stand full of courage in life—trusting in the strength of the Lord.

God's Heart Is
Strong and Courageous

He . . .

⁂ *fights for you.* The father heart of God is strong on your behalf, as "the LORD your God is the one who goes with you to fight for you against your enemies to give you victory" (Deuteronomy 20:4).

⁂ *demonstrates His power on your behalf.* A powerful God knows what you need and stands ready to help in your time of trouble. "O God ... where is there any other as mighty as you? You are the God of miracles and wonders! You still demonstrate your awesome power" (Psalm 77:13-14 TLB).

⁂ *empowers, helps, and upholds you.* Good and loving fathers would never abandon their children or place them in harm's way. Neither will God abandon you! "Don't panic. I'm with you. There's no need to fear for I'm your God. I'll give you strength. I'll help you. I'll hold you steady, keep a firm grip on you" (Isaiah 41:10 THE MESSAGE).

⁂ *is an unfailing protector.* As your children run to you for protection, you, too, have a Protector who is watching out for you. "With God rests my salvation and my glory; He is my Rock of unyielding strength and impenetrable hardness, and my refuge is in God!" (Psalm 62:7 AMP).

29

Into the Jungle

Even today, I can still picture my dad seated on a kapoi—an African carrier—as four men faithfully transported him through the jungles of Africa. It took more stamina than my father possessed to walk for three days straight in the sweltering heat. For sustenance, Mom would tuck several loaves of fresh-baked banana bread into his belongings because it kept longer than most other food items. I can still remember the delicious aroma and looking forward to fresh slices of the tasty treat later.

My courageous dad endured many long trips into the interior of the jungle to preach the gospel despite the unrelenting heat, threats of gorillas, and poisonous snakes. When he would arrive at his destination, the people would mob him, feeling his face, his hair, his arms. They had never seen a white man before. As they stared at this pale creature, they would giggle with childlike delight.

After Dad preached, he would recruit young men from the jungles and bring them back to the mission station. There he trained them to return to their villages and establish their own churches to spread the good news about God's love.

What motivated Dad to take his twenty-six-year-old wife and two young daughters to a mission station in the Belgian Congo? He always told us that one of his favorite Bible verses had inspired him: "Christ's love compels us, because we are convinced that one died for all, and therefore all died" (2 Corinthians 5:14).

Recently, my dad's example encouraged me as I embarked on a mission trip to Brazil. I left the comforts of my American home for a month and traveled to a poor area in Sao Paulo, Brazil, to visit my adopted son Alex. My husband and I had adopted four orphaned, emotionally wounded teenagers and joined with God to nurture them with love and discipline and watch their broken hearts heal. Our Brazilian son had graduated from John Brown University and decided to return to Brazil to help his brothers and sister, who were still living in poverty.

When I sat on my hard bed, which felt like a bag of sand, and studied the tiny bedroom without space to hang my clothes or unpack my suitcase, I thought of my dad venturing into the unknown jungle. Just as he had slept on a cot under the stench of drying elephant meat to share the love of God with those people, I could endure this adjustment to show Christ's love to these emotionally wounded and neglected children. The memory of my dad's bravery gave me courage. As I faced this sacrifice, I grew in my appreciation and admiration of Dad's life of service to the African people.

As I respond to God's call to write and help poor

and needy children, I find myself in need of daily courage. I am grateful for the example of my parents and the courage of my father to press into the unknown to share the love of Christ. His actions taught and inspired me to follow Christ's example more than any words he ever spoke.[2]

A father is a person who growls when
he feels good and laughs very loud when
he's scared half to death.

PAUL HARVEY
American Radio Broadcaster

An Extraordinary Dad Is
Hopeful and Encouraging

A father's encouragement is
the greatest motivational tool on earth.

ANDREA GARNEY
American Author

A father is, in point of fact, the CEO of his family. That may sound powerful, but in reality, it's a tough gig. How can he encourage and uplift others while dealing with so much responsibility—bills, career, the health and welfare of his family? How can he stay upbeat and hopeful for those he loves, even when things aren't going so well in his own life? An extraordinary father realizes that he can't give others what he doesn't have himself. He looks to God for hope and encouragement. He knows that God is invested in his success as he strives to become the best father he can possibly be.

—⁓⁓—

We have put our hope in the living God, who is the Savior of all men, and especially of those who believe.

1 TIMOTHY 4:10

Hope looks for the good instead of harping on the worst.

Hope opens doors where despair closes them.

Hope discovers what can be done instead of grumbling about what cannot.

Hope draws its power from a...deep trust in God....

Hope lights a candle instead of cursing the darkness.

Hope regards problems, small or large, as opportunities. ...

FATHER JAMES KELLER
Founder, the Christophers
1900-1977

Following Father Home

Years ago, when I was jest a little lad,
An' after school hours used to work
Around the farm with Dad,
I used to be so wearied out
When eventide was come,
That I got kinder anxious-like
About the journey home;
But, Dad, he used to lead the way,
An' once in awhile turn 'round an' say,
So cheerin' like, so tender, "Come!
Come on, my son, you're nearly home!"
That allers used to help me some;
An' so I followed Father home.

I'm old an' gray an' feeble now,
An' trembly at the knee,
But life seems just the same today
As then it seemed to me.
For while I am still so wearied out
When eventide is come,
An' still git kinder anxious-like
About the journey home,
But still my Father leads the way,
An' once in awhile I hear Him say,
So cheerin' like, so tender, "Come!
Come on, My son, you're nearly home!"
An' same as then, that helps me some,
And so I'm following Father home.

JOHN TALMAN
Amateur Artist and Draughtsman
1677-1726

A Tribute to My Dad

Now that I have a family of my own, I realize how much my own father carried on his shoulders. And yet, he never complained or sloughed off his responsibilities. When we passed through difficult times, he would encourage us to smile and be confident because God already had the situation under control. What an honor it was to be his child—then and now.

It is my prayer that God would give me the grace to follow in my father's footsteps. That He would show me how to encourage my children to place their trust in Him. I know now what a difficult job it is to be a father. But my dad has proven to me that it can be done right with God's help. And that's where I will place my trust—in Him.

God's Heart Is
Hopeful and Encouraging

He . . .

- *is the God of hope.* As you allow yourself to be filled with the hope of the Father God, you will be able to hope for the best for your children, no matter what situation your family finds itself in. "May the God of hope fill you with all joy and peace as you trust in him, so that you may overflow with hope by the power of the Holy Spirit" (Romans 15:13).

- *has the encouragement you need.* Children long for encouragement from their dads, and your Heavenly Father provides the pattern of encouragement you can follow to encourage your children each day. "He will not break the bruised reed, nor quench the dimly burning flame. He will encourage the fainthearted, those tempted to despair" (Isaiah 42:3 TLB).

- *is on your side.* Is there anything that could come against your children from which you would hesitate to protect them? God is so concerned about the protection of His people that He will do whatever it takes to save them. "If God is for us, who can be against us? He who did not spare his own Son, but gave him up for us all— how will he not also ... graciously give us all things?" (Romans 8:31-32).

Hope for the Battle

It was the middle of the Great Depression when Dad built our little house in the woods near the sawmill where he had finally found a job. He was so upbeat and hopeful that we had made a turnaround. My brother Bill and I loved it there.

But Dad's positive attitude and faith in God would be challenged. One day as I played outside, I found a puddle of something red and sticky on the ground. I knew it was blood!

Mom met me at the door as I came running toward her. "Your brother's bleeding internally," she answered before I could even ask. "You knew he was sick all this week, but he's suddenly become very ill and I don't want you to go near him."

Dad drove into town over the rough logging roads and brought back the country doctor to examine Bill.

"He has typhoid fever," the doctor informed us. "He must have drunk some polluted water in the woods." He told Mom to boil all our drinking water and begin to puree all Bill's food. My brother's bed linens and clothing had to be boiled when they were washed to stem the spread of the disease.

"I'll send out a nurse and she'll give you all typhoid shots, so the rest of you won't get it. She can tell you how to take care of him," the doctor said. "The rest of you are under strict quarantine. And that little girl must not be allowed near her brother. I won't be back. I hope the nurse makes it out here. That logging road's a killer."

The county nurse did come out and gave Mother a list of instructions. "Remember to be careful with his food," she warned. "Typhoid causes the intestinal walls to thin and rupture." The nurse agreed with the doctor that the road was "a killer," and we knew she wouldn't be back either.

The next day my father came home from work with a grim expression on his face—unusual for him. "The sawmill is moving out," he told us. "They're afraid of typhoid fever and I've lost my job."

"What are we to do?" Mom asked.

"Well, your job is to take care of that boy and that's a big job, I know," Dad said. "I'll help where I can, but I'll need to find some way to make money. You're not to worry, Mother. With God's help, we'll make it through this."

Even in the midst of extreme hardship, my father encouraged his family and gave us hope that God would take care of us. The first thing he did was sell the old truck that had brought us all the way to Arkansas. Then a neighbor hired him to cut wood to heat her house that winter. She promised him a dollar a rick. She wasn't afraid of the fever, and she managed to see that Dad was fed a good hot dinner down by the woodpile where he worked. It took him nearly a whole day to cut a rick of wood. He had to fell the trees, split the wood, and cut it into suitable lengths for the kitchen woodstove and the heater.

Then Dad would take his meager earnings and walk seven miles to the nearest town, buy groceries and supplies, and load them on his back for the return trip home.

By Thanksgiving, Bill was feeling better and his fever was down. My grandfather brought a hen for Mom to roast for Thanksgiving dinner, and Bill was able to eat a little dressing.

On Christmas Day, Mom announced, "We have a surprise! Bill is coming out to eat with us."

I was amazed when I saw him. He was nearly bald, because his hair had fallen out from the fever, and he was so thin and frail he could hardly stand up. But his old grin was still there.

I think about the Depression days now and can still clearly remember how often my dad said, "Don't worry, Mother. I'll take care of us."

Dad was a strong man, and with his boundless hope and encouragement, he led us through hard times to better days. His cheery smile seemed to frighten those dark days away.[3]

It is admirable for a man to take his son fishing,
but there is a special place in heaven for the father
who takes his daughter shopping.

JOHN SINOR
American Author

It isn't at all unusual for us to remember,

many years later, words of praise

spoken by our fathers.

They would seem to be written

with indelible ink across the pages

of our hearts and minds.

ANDREA GARNEY
American Author

My father gave me the greatest gift
anyone could give another person;
he believed in me.

JIM VALVANO
College Basketball Coach
1946-1993

—⁓⁓—

You [fathers] hold within your words the power to
help your children feel important and have more
meaningful life experiences.

DOUG FIELDS
Youth Pastor and Author

An Extraordinary Dad
Walks in Wisdom

Wisdom from God shows itself most clearly

in a loving heart.

LLOYD JOHN OGILVIE
Author and Retired Chaplain of the U. S. Senate

My Father ...

When I was four years old, I said:
"My daddy can do anything."

When I was five years old, I said:
"My daddy knows a whole lot."

When I was six years old, I said:
"My dad is smarter than your dad."

When I was eight years old, I said:
"My dad doesn't know exactly everything."

When I was ten years old, I said:
"In the olden days, when my dad grew up,
things were sure different."

When I was twelve years old, I said:
"Oh, well, naturally, my dad doesn't know
anything about that. He's too old to remember
his childhood."

When I was fourteen years old, I said:
"Don't pay any attention to my dad.
He's so old-fashioned."

When I was twenty-one years old, I said:
"Him? Please, he's hopelessly out of date."

When I was twenty-five years old, I said:
"My dad knows about it, but then he should.
He's been around long enough."

When I was thirty years old, I said:
"Maybe I should ask my dad what he thinks.
After all, he's had a lot of experience."

When I was thirty-five years old, I said: "I'm not
doing a single thing until I talk to my dad."

When I was forty years old, I said:
"I wonder how my dad would have handled it.
He was so wise."

When I was fifty years old, I said:
"I'd give anything if my dad were here now
so I could talk to him."

ADAPTED FROM WRITING BY ANN LANDERS

Newspaper Columnist

1918-2002

Extraordinary fathers are wise fathers—not because they have all the answers but because they know where to get the answers. As fathers pick up the mantle of responsibility, they are immediately given the full package of resources they need to shoulder their load. There are no perfect fathers on earth, just regular guys—some more naturally equipped than others, but all with the potential for greatness. All it takes is a willingness to ask for wisdom and then listen carefully to what the Heavenly Father has to say.

—⁓—

Wisdom makes one wise man more powerful than ten rulers in a city.

ECCLESIASTES 7:19

God's Heart Is Full of Wisdom

His Wisdom ...

> • *is freely given.* If your children ask you for advice, do you hesitate to give it to them? God wants the best for you, and He is always willing to give you the wisdom that you need. "If any of you lacks wisdom, he should ask God, who gives generously to all without finding fault, and it will be given to him" (James 1:5).

> • *makes you a vessel of healing.* To be a vessel of healing in your family takes a healthy dose of wisdom that God is willing to provide. "The tongue of the wise brings healing" (Proverbs 12:18).

> • *gives you favor with your boss.* The pressures of leading a family and providing for your children's needs can be overwhelming at times, but God's wisdom will allow you to succeed in every area. "A king delights in a wise servant" (Proverbs 14:35).

> • *gives you discernment.* Raising godly children requires a special dose of wisdom and discernment. God's wisdom is available to every father who seeks it. "The wise in heart are called discerning" (Proverbs 16:21).

> • *makes your home life successful.* A father's wisdom and understanding will create a happy and contented family. "By wisdom a house is built, and through understanding it is established; through knowledge its rooms are filled with rare and beautiful treasures" (Proverbs 24:3-4).

The love, the patience, the kindly wisdom
of a grown man who can enter into the perplexities
and turbulent impulses of a child's heart,
and give cheerful companionship,
and lead by free and joyful ways
to know and choose the things that are pure and
lovely and of good report, make as fair an image
as we can find of that loving, patient Wisdom
which must be above us all.

HENRY VAN DYKE
American Presbyterian Clergyman, Educator, Novelist,
Essayist, Poet, and Religious Writer
1852-1933

*He who is taught to live upon little
owes more to his father's wisdom than
he who has a great deal left him does
to his father's care.*

WILLIAM PENN
English Quaker and Founder of Pennsylvania
1644-1718

A Tribute to My Dad

When I was a child, I thought my father was the smartest man on earth. By the time I was a teenager, I suspected that wasn't true—and I resented him for it. Now I know the truth: my father is wise, and that's much more important than being smart.

I am thankful to the Lord for the father I was given. It is my prayer that God would help me to listen carefully to what my father tells me and retain the advice he gives me. More than that, I desire to develop the same wisdom for my own children—to be more like my dad—having the ability to identify and do those things that are right and pleasing to God.

Taking the High Road

Even as a child, I recognized that my father had a few imperfections, but his wisdom outweighed them all.

The New World Dictionary defines *wisdom* as the "power of judging rightly and following the soundest course of action." By that definition, my father, Hugh Ferguson, was a wise man and certainly the most honest person I have ever known.

I was the youngest of four children, and my father had mellowed a good bit by the time I was born. To my much older siblings, he had been "Father," patterning his actions after his own father—a stern man who displayed few loving feelings. But my father was a "daddy," who no longer shied away from showing his love openly.

I was only eight when Daddy convinced recruiting officers to take him into the Merchant Marines during World War II. Although the father of four and postmaster in our town—a position of respect and responsibility in such a small community—Daddy was a patriot and his country was at war. He had skills that could be used to serve his country, so he volunteered and served as an officer and ship's navigator all over the Pacific.

Even though Daddy felt compelled to serve his country, he still was concerned that his little girl would grow up without his guidance as a father. His solution was to motivate me in long, loving letters to compete for the best grades in school. His letters, written uniquely in green ink and with perfect penmanship, showed me a need to practice my own handwriting skills as I read his wonderful words of wisdom.

I loved Daddy dearly and hated to even disappoint him, much less be a difficult or rebellious daughter, but one day after he came home from the service, I told my father a lie. I was not in the habit of lying to anyone and certainly not to him. I can no longer remember the lie itself but the act of it has stayed with me all these years.

After I told the first lie, I had to tell another to cover it and then a third to cover the first two. After the third, the agony was too great and I had to confess all of them. Doing so was painful for me, but not as painful as the look I saw on my father's face. Still he uttered no angry, chastising words. He wisely chose instead to let me face my wrongdoing and choose honesty for myself. As a result, that experience with dishonesty was my last.

The Bible praises wisdom, according it among the highest of attributes. My father's virtuous life allowed me to say at his funeral that he followed God's pattern of wisdom and "did that which was right in the eyes of the Lord."[4]

My father used to play with my brother and me in the yard. Mother would come out and say, "You're tearing up the grass." "We're not raising grass," my dad would reply, "we're raising boys."

HARMON KILLEBREW
Baseball Hall of Fame First-Base Player

An Extraordinary Dad Is Patient and Understanding

It takes patience to appreciate domestic bliss.

GEORGE SANTAYANA
Philosopher and Author
1863-1952

A Father Means

A Father means so many things—

An understanding heart,

A source of strength and of support

Right from the very start.

A constant readiness to help

In a kind and thoughtful way.

With encouragement and forgiveness

No matter what comes your way.

A special generosity and always affection, too.

A Father means so many things

When he's a man like you.

AUTHOR UNKNOWN

Can't you see the Creator of the universe,

who understands every secret, every mystery ...

sitting patiently and listening to a four-year-old talk to him?

That's a beautiful image of a father.

JAMES C. DOBSON

Christian Psychologist, Author, and Radio Teacher

A father's job is to be patient and understanding with his children—but who is patient and understanding with father? Who comforts him when he's fearful and anxious? Who answers his questions and forgives his mistakes and provides him with wisdom and insight? God does. An extraordinary father realizes that he can pass on only the patience and understanding he has received from his Heavenly Father. When he does that, the whole family celebrates.

―⁓―

A patient man has great understanding.

PROVERBS 14:29

God's Heart Is Patient and Understanding

His patience ...

- *keeps Him from being easily angered.* Godly fathers tap into the patience of God and control their tempers—even as God has compassion on His children, and is full of grace and loving-kindness. "The LORD, the compassionate and gracious God, [is] slow to anger, abounding in love and faithfulness, maintaining love to thousands, and forgiving wickedness, rebellion and sin" (Exodus 34:6-7).

- *gives you time to change, when you need to.* As you trust in God to help you become the father that He wants you to be, He will patiently guide you to see areas in which you can become more like Him. "Many years you were patient with [the children of Israel], and warned them by your spirit through your prophets" (Nehemiah 9:30 NRSV).

His understanding ...

- *is unending.* The Lord has the understanding you need to face every situation! "Great is our Lord, and of great power: his understanding is infinite" (Psalm 147:5 KJV).

- *is coupled with experience through Jesus.* Jesus knows everything you are experiencing this day—and He understands and cares. "We do not have a high priest who is unable to sympathize with our weaknesses, but we have one who has been tempted in every way, just as we are—yet was without sin" (Hebrews 4:15).

A Tribute to My Dad

No one has to tell me that I was a handful when I was growing up. I was the best at doing before thinking, stepping before looking. Most fathers would have been completely out of patience—but not my dad. Sometimes, I'd see him take a deep breath before responding to some new expression of my immaturity. And he would often close his eyes and stand very still for just a moment after snatching me out of harm's way. Now that I'm a parent, I realize just how amazing his patience was.

I want so much to learn the lessons my father taught me about patience and understanding. When my teenager rebels, when my nine-year-old pouts because I've purchased the wrong type of jeans, I want to deal with their childishness without venting frustration. I want to be like my father, Lord, because he was so much like You.

The mark of a good father is his compassionate understanding of the fact that mistakes are a part of growing up.

GARY SMALLEY AND JOHN TRENT
Authors and Experts on Family Relationships

—m—

When he was yet a great way off, his father saw him, and had compassion, and ran, and fell on his neck, and kissed him.

THE PRODIGAL SON
Luke 15:20 KJV

My Heart in His Hands

Nacogdoches, Texas, seemed like a big city to us after moving from a small paper mill community in Michigan with its one-room schoolhouse.

One night that fall, Dad took us to the state fair. Vehicles lined the loading docks of the grain elevators that towered over us menacingly. The lots by the rail yard and the empty warehouses were packed with cars, making the area look like a shopping mall parking lot.

We heard the strange jangle of carnival music as we joined the steady stream of fair-goers headed toward the front gate. Dad pulled out his wallet and paid four dollars apiece for our tickets, seven for his own—an exorbitant price. Muttering to himself as he smoothed a few tired-looking bills back into his billfold, he said, "There are times when a luxury becomes a necessity."

I was shy and reserved, so I clung to Dad's sleeve as he ushered us in. The smells of hot dogs, cotton candy, and popcorn stirred with the sounds of calliope music and the shouts of game hawkers promising stuffed animals and Kewpie dolls assaulted me as we headed down the midway.

A carousel with fantastic horses pranced round and round, flying slowly up and down on their poles. A tiny girl cried as she passed, obviously not appreciating the wonder of the beautiful ride.

"Look there! Don't you want to ride the Ferris wheel?" asked my brother.

"Not yet; I want to get a cotton candy," answered another brother. "Only twenty cents and look how much you get!"

"Well, that's the trick. It just melts away and it's like nothin'. It won't fill you up at all! I tried it before, and boy, was I mad!"

"Who cares? I want one. Smell that?"

I sniffed the sickly sugar sweet air and knew I wanted to taste one of the huge pink fluffs too. In the excitement, I lost track of Dad and followed my brothers to a game booth. My eyes grew wide as the hawker handed them dangerous-looking rifles. One brother climbed up on a step and shot three times—pow! pow! pow!—at the target of swimming ducks, missed, then jumped down, saying, "Maaan! I thought I had it."

Then I saw the whirling lights of the Ferris wheel spinning. Suddenly, it jerked to a halt. A couple of teenaged girls squealed as the wheel stopped, leaving their seat swaying high in the air. How high it looked, how dangerous, and how thrilling!

I ran ahead and grabbed Dad's strong hand. He wasn't afraid of anything. I was safe with him. Then the man stopped and leaned down toward me. "I bet you think I'm your daddy, don't you, little girl?" he asked in a stranger's voice.

I gasped, jerking my fingers from the stranger's

grasp. Where was my daddy? I ran blindly into the crowd ahead, searching desperately for someone I knew. I looked until I found Dad's hand, and when I had made certain that it was connected to his face and his voice, I breathed again.

"What's the matter, sweetie?" he asked. "Something scare you?"

"Nothin'," I choked out in an unconvincing squeak.

Dad squeezed my hand. I felt how strong and warm it was. "There's lots of noise, huh? Well, come on. I'm here." That was Dad. He was always so under-standing—like he knew all about me, all my little quirks, and yet he loved me anyway.

My world was a good place when Dad held my small hand in his big work-roughened one. Nothing could harm me when his laughing voice rang close by. I clung tightly to my father all that evening, but he never pushed me away or snapped at me for pestering him.

When the candied apples were eaten clear down to their sweet juicy sticks and the gates of the fair closed behind us, I was too tired to walk. So Daddy carried me to the car and tucked me gently into the backseat with those wonderful hands. Sighing, I fell asleep in a state of sheer contentment.[5]

A father finds out what is meant by spitting image
when he tries to feed cereal to his infant.

IMOGENE FAY UNDERWOOD

—⁓—

Children are a great comfort in your old age.
And they can help you reach it sooner too.

LIONEL M. KAUFMAN
Author and Educator

An Extraordinary Dad Is Prayerful and Vigilant

As a father, you are your child's

safe harbor in the ocean of life.

PHIL MCGRAW

A Father's Prayer

Dear God, my little child of three
Has said his nightly prayer to Thee;
Before his eyes were closed to sleep
He asked that Thou his soul would keep.
And I, still kneeling at his bed,
My hand upon his tousled head,
Do ask with deep humility,
That Thou, dear Lord, remember me.
Make me, kind Lord, a worthy Dad,
That I may lead this little lad
In pathways ever fair and bright,
That I may keep his steps aright.

O God, his trust must never be

Destroyed or even marred by me.

So, for the simple things he prayed

With childish voice so unafraid,

I, trembling, ask the same from Thee.

Dear Lord, kind Lord, remember me.

AUTHOR UNKNOWN

As children hear their parents praying for wisdom and direction, they learn that parents can't fix everything. I believe God designed it this way. After all, if parents were perfect, children would never sense their need for God.

DR. PAUL MEIER
Psychiatrist and Christian Author

God's Heart Is Prayerful and Vigilant

🕊 *Jesus intercedes for you.* What a comfort for fathers to know! You can count on Jesus to remember your needs and the needs of your children before the Father. "[Jesus] is able to save completely those who come to God through him, because he always lives to intercede for them" (Hebrews 7:25).

🕊 *The Holy Spirit prays God's will.* Many situations that fathers face are difficult to understand or even pray for. But the Holy Spirit can pray, on your behalf, the perfect will of God. "We do not know what we ought to pray for, but the Spirit himself intercedes for us with groans that words cannot express. ... The Spirit intercedes for the saints in accordance with God's will" (Romans 8:26-27).

🕊 *God watches over you.* No human father can watch over his children every moment of the day, but your Heavenly Father stands guard, even when you cannot. "He will not let your foot slip—he who watches over you will not slumber ... nor sleep. The LORD watches over you—the LORD is your shade at your right hand; the sun will not harm you by day, nor the moon by night. The LORD will keep you from all harm—he will watch over your life; the LORD will watch over your coming and going both now and forevermore" (Psalm 121:3-8).

A Tribute to My Dad

I will never forget the sense of peace and security I felt when hearing my father pray. When we were sick, he prayed. When we misbehaved, he prayed. When we needed something, he prayed. He prayed for us when we left the house in the morning and before we fell asleep at night. At meals, we waited, unwilling to even pick up our forks—until our father prayed.

Heavenly Father,

Now, Lord, I pray for my father. I ask You to strengthen his aging body and mind. I ask You to meet his needs and fill his heart and mind with peace and joy. I ask You to bless his food and give him rest when he sleeps. And I thank You, Lord, for a father whose prayers have molded my life.

AMEN.

"Wait Till Your Father Gets Home!"

I was being rotten that day. Utterly rotten, as only a very determined eight-year-old can be. And I didn't even care.

I fought with my sisters. I fought with my brothers. And now I refused to do the dishes.

"Every single night I do them!" I yelled. "Every single night of my life! I'm only eight years old! I work at school all day long. I shouldn't have to work at home too. So I'm just not going to!"

Of course, I selfishly ignored the fact that my poor mother was doing all the cooking and sewing and cleaning for my father and five children—with another on the way—plus the dishes from the other two meals. She needed my older sister and me to do the evening dishes, so she could bathe the youngest ones and put them to bed.

"All right, young lady!" Mother said. "You just wait till your father gets home!"

So? Daddy loved learning and school too. Surely he would see that those were the most important things in life … and that the dishes were Mother's job, not mine.

My father worked hard six days a week. By the time he reached home after a long commute, he was weary. All he wanted was a meal, a newspaper, and a couch to collapse on. Instead, he got me. His usual jovial face was stern.

"Bonnie, what's this about not doing the dishes for your poor mother?" he asked.

"Well, it's not my job!" I protested. "She can just do them herself if she wants them done! I don't have to do everything around here!"

He shook his head. "Young lady, if you don't go right in there and apologize to your poor mother and do what she says, I'm going to have to punish you."

Now I was feeling uneasy. But still stubborn. "No. It's her fault. She shouldn't make me!"

He shook his head again. "All right," he sighed. "You give me no choice. You will be spending the evening in your room—without dinner, without television."

My face drained. But I still wasn't going to back down. Let him hold me prisoner! I'll call the police! I'll tell my teacher! Jumping up, I ran into my room and threw myself on my bed. Obviously, no one loved me or they wouldn't treat me like this! I'd just stay there and cry for the rest of my life.

The longer I lay there, the louder my sobs sounded. But suddenly, I realized something strange. I could hear someone else's voice—even above the din of my own exaggerated crying.

I held my breath and listened. It was my father—praying for me. I felt so ashamed.

The next morning no one mentioned what had happened the night before. But I never refused to do the dishes again. And my father never punished me again. He never had to. His prayers prevailed.[6]

When Father Prays

When father prays he doesn't use
The words the preacher does;
There's different things for different days,
But mostly it's for us.

When father prays the house is still,
His voice is slow and deep.
We shut our eyes, the clock ticks loud,
So quiet we must keep.

Sometimes the prayer gets very long
And hard to understand,
And then I wiggle up quite close,
And let him hold my hand.

I can't remember all of it,
I'm little yet, you see;
But one thing I cannot forget,
My father prays for me!

AUTHOR UNKNOWN

When I was a kid,
I used to imagine animals running under my bed.
I told my dad, and he solved the problem
by cutting off the legs of the bed.

LOU BROCK
One of the Greatest Base Stealers
in Major League Baseball History

The thing to remember about fathers is,
they're men. A girl has to keep it in mind:
They are dragon-seekers, bent on improbable
rescues. Scratch any father, you find someone
chock-full of qualms and romantic terrors,
believing change is a threat—like your first shoes
with heels on, like your first bicycle it took such
months to get.

PHYLLIS MCGINLEY
Leading American Author of Light Verse
1905-1978

An Extraordinary Dad
Gives of Himself

The best gift a father can give his child is
the gift of himself—his time. For material things
mean little if there is not someone
to share them with.

C. NEIL STRAIT
Pastor and Author
1934-2003

Only a Dad

Only a dad, with a tired face

Coming home at night from the daily race

Bringing little of gold or fame,

To show how well he has played the game;

But glad in his heart that his own rejoice

To see him come and to hear his voice.

Only a dad, with a brood of four,

One of ten million men or more.

Plodding along in the daily strife,

Bearing the whips and the scorns of life,

With never a whimper of pain or hate,

For the sake of those who back home await.

Only a dad, neither rich nor proud,

Merely one of the milling crowd,

Toiling, striving, from day to day,

Facing whatever may come his way,

Silent, whenever the harsh condemn,

And bearing it all for the love of them.

Only a dad, but he gives his all,

To smooth the way for his children small,

Doing, with courage stern and grim

The deeds that his father did for him.

This is the line that for him I pen:

Only a dad, but the best of men.

EDGAR ALBERT GUEST
American Writer
1881-1959

If a child is to keep his inborn sense of wonder,
he needs the companionship of at least one
adult who can share it, rediscovering with him
the joy, excitement, and mystery
of the world we live in.

RACHEL CARSON
American Marine Biologist and Science Writer
1907-1964

God's Heart Gives of Himself

- *Through Jesus, He serves you*—and Jesus is the example for all fathers to follow in giving to their families. "The Son of Man did not come to be served, but to serve, and to give his life as a ransom for many" (Matthew 20:28).

- *Through Jesus, He treats you like a friend and shares His heart with you.* How wonderful it is when fathers and children go beyond their natural relationship and become friends! The heart of God also longs for friendship with His children. Jesus said, "Greater love has no one than this, that he lay down his life for his friends. You are my friends if you do what I command. I no longer call you servants, because a servant does not know his master's business. Instead, I have called you friends, for everything that I learned from my Father I have made known to you. You did not choose me, but I chose you" (John 15:13-16).

- *He stays faithful to you, no matter what.* Would you ever deny your children? Your faithfulness to them is just a small reflection of the Father's faithfulness to you. "If we are faithless, He remains faithful; He cannot deny Himself" (2 Timothy 2:13 NKJV).

A Tribute to My Dad

It would be impossible to calculate the sacrifices my father has made on my behalf. All my life he has put his family first. He excused himself from a meeting at the office to attend my parent/teacher conference, bought a less expensive car so he could pay for my braces, spent his evenings helping me do my math homework even when he was tired. I always knew he loved me.

Now it's my turn in life to make some sacrifices for my father. As I look to God for guidance, I want to make his life easier, encourage him, let him know that I love him and appreciate all he has done for me. It is the very least I can do to honor a man who gave his all for his family.

Fathers have to be great jugglers. Not only are they asked to give themselves completely to their families, they must also be careful to properly balance their work life (providing for their families) with their home life (being with their families). It's a daunting task.

Extraordinary fathers don't try to perfect this juggling act on their own. They look to God for wisdom and stamina, and in the process, they often find some time for themselves.

—∿—

The desires of the diligent are fully satisfied.

PROVERBS 13:4

Spelling L-O-V-E

"Betty! Bonnie! Bob! Paula!"

I blinked awake. The house that a moment before slumbered in early-Saturday-morning darkness was now alive with lights and groggy children.

I pulled the covers back over my head. But it was no use. Daddy had brought us his usual Saturday-morning offering of love.

"Good morning, girls!" he boomed. Already dressed for his half-day Saturday's work, he glowed in cardboard-stiff white shirt, rosy cheeks, prematurely silver hair, and beaming smile.

"Here, Bonnie, this is your list of words for this morning. Betty, here's yours. If you learn them right away, you can have some more before I go!"

For in our home, the delightful, carefree wonder of Saturday began, not with a chance to sleep in for a spell, but with spelling itself. As in s-p-e-l-l-i-n-g.

Protests got us nowhere. "Don't worry, children," Daddy would assure us cheerfully. "You'll thank me when you're older. I wish I could have done this when I was your age." And, believe it or not, he meant it!

Harold Compton's love affair with learning began as a precocious four-year-old. Every morning his father, Charlie, left their hardscrabble farm in the hills of

Eastern Kentucky for his teaching post at a nearby hamlet.

The schoolmaster's lot back then was a lonely, hard, and poorly paid one. But to his young son, getting to spend the day in a world of books instead of chores seemed the ultimate luxury. Eventually, Harold's persistent begging broke down his weary father's resolve. After that, Charlie's faithful mule carried both father and son off in the predawn darkness. And soon Harold was blissfully immersed in the "Three R's"— Reading, 'Riting, and 'Rithmetic.

Devouring every book available, young Harold dreamed of high school and Latin and Greek and Shakespeare and college. And all the wonders such an education would bring.

Then tragedy: his beloved father died. And, in quick succession, so did two brothers and a sister.

As new head of his family, Harold had four funeral debts to pay and a large family of brothers and sisters to feed. This meant leaving school after the eighth grade for twelve hours a day, six days a week of back-breaking, unskilled labor in fields and forests for fifty cents a day.

But he never gave up his dream. And years later, bypassing high school altogether, he went on to a teachers' training college and became a teacher himself. Eventually he left the hills and hollows of Eastern

Kentucky for the bustling cities of Chicago and
Cincinnati, as a highly skilled building estimator. World
War II brought an end to the housing industry.
Immediately Harold became part of the even-more-
booming defense industry.

Then peace. And suddenly he was out of work, his
lungs filled with metal shavings. Thus, twenty years
after Harold left that Kentucky hollow, he found
himself back in it, in poor health, and with a new
family of children to care for—his own.

Even there, though, in our tumbledown log cabin,
near where he himself had grown up, he kept his dream
alive. For crowded around its 150-year-old fireplace
were our treasures: a piano, crammed-full bookcases, a
well-thumbed Bible, and a weighty Merriam-Webster's
unabridged dictionary.

Besides running the farm, both he and my mother
taught in schools much like the ones they themselves
attended as children and taught in as young adults.

Even there, busy as we were, our Saturday morning
spellings continued. And so did Harold's self-education.
For he pored over that dictionary at night by kerosene-
light, after the last chores were done, memorizing word
by word.

Nor was that all. When he plowed or harrowed his
rock-strewn fields, he grandly orated full Latin
conjugations to his startled mules. For he had finally

taught himself Latin, too, from the hand-me-down textbooks we children used in high school.

We were still dirt-poor when my older sister, Betty, graduated from high school. Determined that she continue her education, Daddy drove her to Georgetown College himself in our wired-together '37 Chevy. Admitting that he didn't have a penny to put on her account, he promised the school that if she was accepted, he and Mother would pay all her bills somehow.

Many a night we would wake up to hear Daddy and Mother praying over how to make ends meet. But eventually all four of us went to college. And all of the bills were paid. We never dared give up, even at our most discouraged. Daddy was counting on us to make it.

By the way, those Saturday mornings "took." From them we learned a world of words that helped one sister become a journalist, another a teacher, another a writer, a brother a lawyer.

But the word we learned best was: L-O-V-E.[7]

You can do anything with children
if you only play with them.

OTTO VON BISMARCK
Prussian Statesman
1815-1898

My father didn't do anything unusual.
He only did what dads are supposed to do—be there.

MAX LUCADO
Minister and One of Christianity's Most Popular Authors

———ᴍ———

In everything I did, I showed you that
by this kind of hard work we must help the weak,
remembering the words the Lord Jesus himself said:
"It is more blessed to give than to receive."

ACTS 20:35

An Extraordinary Dad Leads by Example

What we desire our children to become,

we must endeavor to be before them.

ANDRE COMBE
Scottish Physiologist
1797-1847

Leading by example places power behind the positive. It says: "This is the right way. See how well it works?" While a child might question your words, the demonstration of positive action and its resulting outcome reside beyond the realm of the theoretical—tucked securely into the reality of everyday living. Extraordinary fathers practice the power of positive example. No wonder their children celebrate them.

—⁓—

Be an example to them of good deeds
of every kind. Let everything you do reflect
your love of the truth.

Titus 2:7 tlb

Every father is to be the instructor and living example for his children in obeying the commands of God and the teachings of Jesus.

CATHERINE MARSHALL
Beloved American Fiction Writer
1915-1983

Celebrate Dad

I'd rather see a sermon

Than hear one any day;

I'd rather one should walk with me

Than merely tell the way.

EDGAR A. GUEST

Poet and Newspaperman

1881-1959

God's Heart Leads by Example

The Heavenly Father illustrated through Jesus what it means to lead by example. Fathers must follow this example and demonstrate the love of God to their children.

- "When [Jesus] had finished washing their feet, he put on his clothes and returned to his place. 'Do you understand what I have done for you?' he asked them. 'You call me "Teacher" and "Lord," and rightly so, for that is what I am. Now that I, your Lord and Teacher, have washed your feet, you also should wash one another's feet. I have set you an example that you should do as I have done for you'" (John 13:12-15).

- "Husbands, love your wives, just as Christ loved the church and gave himself up for her to make her holy, cleansing her by the washing with water through the word, and to present her to himself as a radiant church, without stain or wrinkle or any other blemish, but holy and blameless. In this same way, husbands ought to love their wives as their own bodies. He who loves his wife loves himself. After all, no one ever hated his own body, but he feeds and cares for it, just as Christ does the church" (Ephesians 5:25-29).

- Jesus said, "As the Father has loved me, so have I loved you. Now remain in my love. If you obey my commands, you will remain in my love, just as I have obeyed my Father's commands and remain in his love. I have told you this so that my joy may be in you and that your joy may be complete. My command is this: Love each other as I have loved you" (John 15:9-12).

A Tribute to My Dad

When I was a teenager, I sometimes looked at my friends' fathers and wondered what it would be like to be someone else's child—someone willing to bend the rules occasionally, someone a little less focused about issues of right and wrong. Now that I'm grown, though, I cherish my father's fiery passion for godliness. I've watched him all of my life and he's never wavered from his faith and commitment to God.

I see now that his example has taught me that I can do the right thing—no matter how difficult that might be. I can place my life in God's hands and trust Him to guide me according to His perfect will and purpose. My father's example has taught me that I can be all God created me to be. I am so thankful to the Lord for my father and for the blessing he has brought down upon the heads of his children.

A person who lives right and is right has more power in his silence than another has by words.

PHILLIPS BROOKS
Episcopal Bishop
1835-1893

———

Keep yourself clean and bright—you are the window through which your children see God.

AUTHOR UNKNOWN

Safely Home

I was seven years old when the big blizzard came howling across the Dakota plains. That morning as my brother Bill and I bundled up and hauled out our shiny new skis to go to school, we were delighted with the day. The sun had shone briefly the day before, melting the snow enough to leave an icy crust on the surface. We skimmed over the drifts, light as birds flying.

We attended a small country school, two miles from our house by road and a mile and a half when we cut across the fields. Our teacher Miss Gray met us in the little entryway, checking for frostbite before she let us go in to stand by the roaring fire in the heater.

"Nose and ears are red as beets," she laughed. "But you're fine. Your mother wrapped you up warmly."

There were fifteen students enrolled in the school, but only thirteen were there that day. I was the youngest, and Helen was the eldest, a stocky competent eighth-grader, who helped Miss Gray with the younger children.

We moved the benches into a circle around the coal stove, and Helen put her raw potatoes into the hot ashes to bake for lunch. "I'm baking one for you too," she whispered, and I grinned my thanks.

By recess time the room was still cold, and the teacher told us we were to stay inside. My friend and I were coloring when the telephone rang, startling us.

"Call the parents," a rough voice announced. "Get the children home as quickly as possible. A bad storm is coming and moving fast."

We were quickly bundled into our coats and mufflers, our ski pants and boots. Within minutes parents arrived to hurry their children into their sleighs and head for home. Soon only Helen and her brother and Bill and I were left. Then the door flew open and my wonderful father burst in on a gust of wind and snow.

"I can't get the Martins," cried Miss Gray. "Their phone line must be down."

"I'll take them home," said Dad. "Their house is not too far out of the way. How about you? Is someone coming for you? There's room in our sleigh. We pass your place on the way to the Martins."

"Thank you so much," Miss Gray said. "I hadn't even thought of myself yet." I was so proud of my father!

Dad had filled the bed of the sleigh with wheat straw covered with a huge buffalo-skin robe, and he urged us to lie down in the straw under the robe. Miss Gray objected, saying, "I'll ride up front with you."

But Dad said, "No, you'll do no such thing. The wind is fierce!" So Dad covered us all with the heavy buffalo skin, and we were off.

I was snug and warm, filled with delight at the thought of going home early. I scarcely noticed when Dad helped Miss Gray into her house, or Helen and her brother out of the sleigh. I snuggled down in the straw with Bill, deeply content. My father would take us safely home.

But Dad was having trouble. He later told us, "When we turned away from the Martins, the blizzard suddenly got worse. The wind almost knocked me down and the snow got so thick I couldn't see the horses' heads. They were still moving, struggling though the drifts. I knew we were only a mile from home, but I couldn't tell where I was, whether we were going toward home or away from it. All I could do was let the reins go slack and let the horses find their way home. I prayed! Oh, Lord, how I prayed!"

Was it merely instinct that guided the powerful team through the blinding storm? No, it was much more than that. God's hand was on them in their gallant struggle, leading us all to warmth and safety.

"They're a good team," said Dad, "but it was God who brought us home."

Since then, there have been times when I've faced trouble and felt totally lost and bewildered. I wish I could say that I've always had the serenity and trust of the little girl under the buffalo robe.

Still, looking back, I can say that my father's example of plowing forward, despite the circumstances, and taking care of others has always been a model for me. Neither my father nor God ever failed me. They always brought me safely home.[8]

Children are unpredictable.
You never know what inconsistency
they're going to catch you in next.

FRANKLIN P. JONES
American Businessman
1887-1929

Your children see through your example
that God can use them in spite of,
or perhaps because of, their failings.

AUTHOR UNKNOWN

I watched a small man with thick calluses on
both hands work fifteen and sixteen hours a day. I
saw him once literally bleed from the bottoms of his
feet, a man who came here uneducated, alone,
unable to speak the language, who taught me all I
needed to know about faith and hard work by the
simple eloquence of his example.

MARIO CUOMO
Former New York Governor

An Extraordinary Dad Points His Children to God

What God is to the world,
a father is to his children.

PHILO JUDAEUS
Alexandrian Philosopher
20 B.C. - c. 40 A.D.

A Father's Place

It is a father's place
To be concerned about his own,
His household's faith in God;
The love of Christ enthrone.

It is a father's place
Today and every day
To read the Word in circle sweet,
And lead and guide and pray.

Will you be one of those
To take his proper place?
To sit at meat with grateful heart,
His table, in Christ, grace?

Oh, Christian fathers!

Hear God's Word! His voice to obey!

And, thereby, teach your families

To love and trust and pray.

Eva Gray

Actress

*We teach our children to call God Father,
and the only conception of fatherhood that they
can have is the conception that we give them.
Human fatherhood should be molded
and modeled on the pattern of the
fatherhood of God.*

WILLIAM BARCLAY
Scottish Scholar
1907-1978

God's Heart Leads Them to Himself

As a father, your most important accomplishment will be to introduce your children to their Heavenly Father, who loves them far more than you will ever be able to love them.

- *He draws you to himself.* He says, "Yes, I have loved you with an everlasting love; therefore with lovingkindness I have drawn you" (Jeremiah 31:3 NKJV).

- *He arranges things so you will seek Him.* "From one man he made every nation of men, that they should inhabit the whole earth; and he determined the times set for them and the exact places where they should live. God did this so that men would seek him and perhaps reach out for him and find him, though he is not far from each one of us" (Acts 17:26-27).

- *He enables you to find Him.* "'You will seek me and find me when you seek me with all your heart. I will be found by you,' declares the Lord" (Jeremiah 29:13-14).

- *He leads you through Jesus.* Jesus said, "I am the way, the truth, and the life. No one comes to the Father except through Me" (John 14:6 NKJV).

- *He lights your way through Jesus.* Jesus said, "I am the light of the world. Whoever follows me will never walk in darkness, but will have the light of life" (John 8:12).

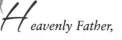

*H*eavenly Father,

Knowing You want me to have a relationship, with my children, that is characterized by the fruit of patience and kindness, show me ways in which I can bless them with kind words and loving actions. Show me creative ways to spend quality and meaningful time with my children.

During those times when anger would be the easiest reaction, help me respond with a kind tone of voice and a pleasant expression on my face. And, allow that kindness to draw us together.

In those moments of frustration and stress, help me to be patient. Teach me ways that I can exemplify honor, courage, and Godly strength to my family, so that we might build a meaningful and lifelong bond together.

AMEN.

The most important job a father has is to introduce his children to their Heavenly Father. Though he may fall short in many other ways, the father who does this has handed his children the golden key to life—a living relationship with the God who created them. Such a father will be praised and celebrated both here and in eternity.

The LORD's love for those who respect him continues forever and ever, and his goodness continues to their grandchildren.

PSALM 103:17 NCV

The Tonka Truck

Dad punched the drunkard out and left him lying on the front walk until the cops could come and rake him up and haul him off to jail. The man, who had previously been evicted from our rental house, had come barging into our home, screeching, "This is my place! My place, you hear—so get out!"

Soon we were able to buy a house on the river and move. Dad had started going to a local Baptist church and things were changing in our family. His rebellious heart turned to God and the change was real. He decided to quit smoking, replacing the cigarette pack in his pocket with candy, lemon drops, and root beer barrels, which made him popular with us kids!

Dad was truly changed. No more movie-going for us. Playing cards was out—no more gambling. He deliberated over dice and decided that we could keep those in board games like Monopoly, Uncle Wiggly, and Candyland.

But fun was never outlawed. We had plenty—birthday parties, company, canoe trips, family camp, and Sunday school picnics. Dad played with us, and he was the happiest we had ever known him.

Still, the enemy knew Dad's weakness was his temper, and so he worked overtime to see that Dad would have ample opportunity to fight. A situation with an irate neighbor soon evolved into a feud. The neighbor claimed he had right-of-way across our land to the riverbank. When Dad built a fence, Mr. Zack tore it down and drove his truck through the yard. Dad put the fence back up, but our neighbor tore it down again.

The third time landed their dispute in court where the judge laid out a compromise. Mr. Zack could have access, but he had to leave the fence and build another road that didn't cross the yard.

A large blustery man and a drinker with a lazy lifestyle and a poverty-stricken family, Mr. Zack soon built his road of sand and gravel and topped it with cinders, which were sharp and miserable to step on.

One warm spring day my brothers were playing in the leftover sand pile with their Tonka truck. Scooping up sand, they would fill the bed of the truck, drive it across the pile, and raise the tiny steel bar that dumped the load.

Then Mr. Zack drove up. He slammed his truck door and screamed at the boys. "Get out of my sand! Who do you think you are? That's my sand, now git!"

The boys scrambled for cover and only looked back to see Mr. Zack toss their Tonka truck into the back of his pickup.

When Dad arrived home and heard about the encounter, he went straight back to the car and headed to the Zack's to confront the bully. He drove around the lake and down the dirt road beside the town dump to their drive, back through a stand of pine trees, planning to take care of the situation once and for all.

But when he turned in the drive, he spotted a small boy, about five years old, sitting in the dirt. "Hey! Look, Mister. Look what I got and it ain't even Christmas!" he yelled, jumping up and pointing at the yellow dump truck. "It really dumps too. Watch, Mister!"

"Where'd you get it?" asked Dad, knowing the answer.

"My dad brought it for me today. Ain't it a good one?"

"Sure is, son," Dad answered. He rolled up his window, backed out of the drive, and drove home slowly. Still, Mama was surprised to see him back so soon.

"What happened, Larry?"

"Nothing," he said. "His boy was out playing with the truck. Probably the first toy his dad ever gave him. I couldn't tell him his dad stole it. I couldn't take it from the kid."

Dad's heart of vengeful anger had been removed and replaced with one pulsing with compassion. I imagined the boy playing happily with the truck and it being his first toy ever.

Over the years Dad continued to teach us about God, saying, "Kill your old man off, your old sinful mean self, and become a new person inside. That's what being 'born again' means."

Every night at the supper table, Dad read the Bible to us. He carried us to Sunday school and Bible camp and prayed with and for us. He taught us through his own actions what Christ looks like and pointed us toward God.[9]

The greatest gift I ever had came from God and I call him "Dad."

AUTHOR UNKNOWN

—⁓—

*It's only when you grow up,
and step back from him, or leave him for your own
career and your own home—it's only then that
you can measure his greatness and fully
appreciate it. Pride reinforces love.*

MARGARET TRUMAN
Popular American Author and Daughter
of President Harry Truman

ENDNOTES

1. Kathryn Lay, Arlington, Texas. Used by permission of the author.

2. Sharon Gibson, Siloam Springs, Arkansas. Used by permission of the author.

3. Margaret Maghe, Okmulgee, Oklahoma. Used by permission of the author.

4. Trudy Graham, Tulsa, Oklahoma. Used by permission of the author.

5. Elece Hollis, Boynton, Oklahoma. Used by permission of the author.

6. Bonnie Compton Hanson, Santa Ana, California. Used by permission of the author.

7. Bonnie Compton Hanson, Santa Ana, California. Used by permission of the author.

8. Margaret Maghe, Okmulgee, Oklahoma. Used by permission of the author.

9. Lisa Brink, Boynton, Oklahoma. Used by permission of the author.

This and other titles in the *Celebration Series*
are available from your local bookstore.

Celebrate Love
Celebrate the Graduate
Celebrate Mom

If this book has touched your life,
we would love to hear from you.
Please send your correspondence to:
Editorialdept@whitestonebooks.com
Visit our website at:
www.whitestonebooks.com

*"... To him who overcomes I will give some of the hidden manna to
eat. And I will give him a white stone, and on the stone a new name
written which no one knows except him who receives it."*

REVELATION 2:17 NKJV

WHITE STONE BOOKS
LAKELAND, FLORIDA